Bull Trout's Gift

Bull Trout's Gift

A Salish Story about the Value of Reciprocity

Confederated Salish and Kootenai Tribes
Illustrated by Sashay Camel

UNIVERSITY OF NEBRASKA PRESS | LINCOLN & LONDON

This project is made possible through the generous support of the
Confederated Salish and Kootenai Tribes' Jocko River Restoration Fund.

Library of Congress Cataloging-in-Publication Data

Bull trout's gift : a Salish story about the value of reciprocity /
Confederated Salish and Kootenai Tribes ; illustrated by Sashay Camel.
p. cm.
ISBN 978-0-8032-3491-8 (cloth : alk. paper)
1. Salish Indians—Folklore—Juvenile literature. 2. Bull trout—Legends—
Juvenile literature. I. Camel, Sashay, ill. II. Confederated Salish &
Kootenai Tribes of the Flathead Reservation, Montana.
E99.S2B85 2011   398.208997'9435—dc22
2010046045

To our elders and ancestors, who teach us that when you take from the land,
you must give something in return, a gift of equal or greater value.

To our children, who will inherit this place we call home.

And to Bull Trout. Thank you.

Contents

Acknowledgments

The Confederated Salish and Kootenai Tribal Fisheries Program enthusiastically supported this project. We want to thank Tom McDonald, Les Evarts, and Craig Barfoot, who early on recognized the power that education can play in environmental restoration. We thank Johnny Arlee, Craig Barfoot, and Ronda Howlett and her students for participating in the project.

Bull Trout's Gift

"Field Trip Day!"

Those were the three words everyone was speaking in Ms. Howlett's class that morning in September. Ms. Howlett and her class were on their way to the Jocko River to learn how to restore a stream.

To reach the river, Ms. Howlett's class only had to walk about fifteen minutes. But because the kids in the class came from all over the valley, many of them had never been there, at least not to stand on the river's banks. The closest they had come was to drive across one of the two highway bridges that cross the river. But there were a handful, perhaps a third of the class, who had grown up on the banks of the Jocko, fishing and swimming in its pools, building forts in the cottonwoods and pines on its banks, and sometimes crossing it on the enormous downed trees that occasionally drop across it.

"Class," Ms. Howlett said, "quiet! It's time to go to the river. Grab your lunches, and don't forget your journals." Out the door they went into a bright September day, the sky as blue as the forget-me-nots that grow on the river's banks.

The Jocko River—all fifty miles of it—flows through the Flathead Indian Reservation in northwestern Montana. For thousands of years the Salish and Pend d'Oreille Indians lived along the river.

The river provided everything the people needed to lead good lives. From the river's banks they harvested plants of all kinds for food and medicine. From its waters they caught bull trout and cutthroat trout and whitefish. On its floodplain they hunted white-tailed deer, mule deer, elk and grouse, ducks and geese.

Often they camped along the river, and wherever they camped they smoked and dried meat, processed plant foods, played games, told stories, danced, sang, built sweathouses, and prayed. They called the Jocko River, with its clear waters and abundant food, their home.

Just over one hundred years ago the valley began to change. The government in Washington, D.C., opened the Flathead Indian Reservation to settlement by non-Indians. Gradually new people arrived in the valley to claim land.

They built ranches, railroads, highways, and towns. Where the river was in the way, they moved it and straightened its meanders. They cleared large areas of the floodplain of native vegetation and replaced it with crops or grass. They took water from the river to irrigate, so much water that at certain times of the year the river dried up in places. They grazed cattle—thousands of them—on the floodplain, all the way from the river's headwaters to its mouth. They logged the mountains above the river, sometimes clearcutting tens of thousands of square miles. Between the towns they built homes, some right on the river. They built bridges, dikes, levees, and canals.

In the Jocko itself they introduced fish: not native species, but non-native fish from other parts of the world—species like rainbow trout, brown trout, and brook trout. In short, the twentieth century changed the Jocko River, its fish and wildlife, and the Salish and Pend d'Oreille people.

Now Ms. Howlett's class was on its way to a part of the river that the tribes of the reservation—the Salish, Pend d'Oreille, and Kootenai—were spending millions of dollars to restore. They were mending a twenty-two-mile stretch of the river so native fish and wildlife could once again thrive and so the members of the Tribes could continue their traditions.

At the river, Mr. Johnny Arlee, a tribal elder, and Mr. Craig Barfoot, one of the biologists in charge of restoration, joined the class. Each of the students found a big rock or log to sit on; in front of them, catbirds, yellow warblers, orioles, dippers, and a host of other birds sang.

Over the sounds of the river Ms. Howlett said, "Mr. Barfoot wants to talk with you about what makes a healthy stream."

Mr. Barfoot, the fisheries biologist, stood to speak. "A healthy river is what we all want, but how do we get that? Probably the simplest way is to stop doing the things that harm the river and let the river heal itself, which it will do over time. It is a process we can speed up somewhat by paying attention to four words," he said, "and those words all start with a C: cold, clean, complex, and connected. Streams that are healthy for native fish and wildlife are cold, clean, complex, and connected. Let's talk about each of those words."

"Cold: The native trout in the river—bull trout and cutthroat trout—and the insects that feed them can only thrive in cold water. Streams stay much colder when they are shaded by trees and shrubs. So to keep streams cold we need to protect the riparian area—the ribbon of trees and shrubs that grows along the river. If the riparian area is protected from clearing and weeds it will grow tall enough to shade the river."

"Clean: Clean streams have clean water and clean gravel bottoms. Native trout need clean gravel to spawn. Sediment—soil and silt that washes into the stream—smothers trout eggs and kills them. Many aquatic insects also need clean gravel. And, of course, people need clean water for drinking, swimming, and other things.

"Riparian areas should be kept clean because in the spring, high water spreads onto the floodplain and can carry whatever is there into the river. Garbage, cow manure, oil, and other chemicals can harm fish and wildlife and have no place in the riparian area of a healthy river."

"Complex: A complex stream has lots of different types of habitats, such as pools, riffles, runs, and glides; lots of shade and undercut banks; and lots of logs in the stream. Each kind of habitat provides something trout need; each is part of a healthy stream. Streams will become complex over time if they are left alone.

"It is also important that riparian areas are complex. Complex riparian areas have tall trees, medium-sized trees, and short trees. They have lots and lots of different species of shrubs and herbs and grasses. They have dense thickets and open areas. Complex riparian areas have many different types of habitat, and that means more wildlife."

"Connected: Healthy streams are connected to the floodplain. That means during floods, water is able to flow not only in the stream channel but also over the banks and onto the floodplain, where it soaks into the ground to become groundwater. Then, later, when things get hot and dry in summer, that groundwater is available for the riparian plants that live on the floodplain, and that helps wildlife.

"A healthy riparian area also helps fish. When flows in the river get low, like they do in late summer, the groundwater flows back into the river. It keeps the water level in the stream high enough so that the fish and insects don't dry out and die. Because the groundwater is cold, it cools the river, which also helps the fish. For the Jocko River to be a healthy stream it needs to be connected to its floodplain."

Lake Pend Oreille

Flathead Lake

Clark Fork River

Flathead River

Jocko River

A Bull Trout's Journey

Every year, bull trout migrated to and from the headwaters of the Jocko River to Lake Pend Oreille, 175 miles away.

"But 'connected' has another meaning, too. Trout spend different stages of their lives in different parts of a river system. They spawn in one part, grow up in another, and live as adults in another. Each of these different living places can be thought of as a link in a chain. Each provides something the fish need. When the chain is broken, even if it's just a single link, the trout population will suffer.

"Before dams were built on the Clark Fork River, some Jocko River bull trout traveled all the way down the Jocko River and into the Flathead River. From there they swam downstream to the Clark Fork River and then on to Lake Pend Oreille, a distance of over 175 miles. Later, those same fish traveled upstream all the way back to the Jocko to spawn. These bull trout were called migratory bull trout because they traveled out of the Jocko River. They grew large—up to twenty-seven inches long. The biggest ones weighed over twenty pounds. Now, because of the dams that block the river, those fish can't travel to and from Lake Pend Oreille, and that kind of migratory bull trout has disappeared from the Jocko River."

"There is another kind of migratory bull trout that still visits the Jocko River. Instead of spending its adult life in a large lake like Lake Pend Oreille, it spends it in a large river, in this case both the Flathead River and the Clark Fork River. These trout return to the Jocko to spawn, and like the bull trout that once migrated to Lake Pend Oreille, they get big, often over two feet long. There used to be thousands of these fish returning to the Jocko every fall to spawn. Now there are just a few. That's because the Jocko and the Flathead Rivers are not as cold, clean, complex, or connected as they used to be.

"A third kind of bull trout also lives in the Jocko River. It's called a resident bull trout, and it never leaves the Jocko. It is born here, grows up here, spawns here, and dies here. Resident bull trout tend to be small; they rarely get any longer than twelve inches. Like migratory bull trout, they are not doing well. They used to live throughout the river. Now you can only find them in a few places because the Jocko River is not as cold, clean, complex, or connected as it used to be.

"Those are some of the most important things that make a healthy river," Mr. Barfoot said, as he sat back down with the students.

"I think now it's time to hear what Johnny has to tell us about the Jocko," Ms. Howlett said, and she asked Johnny Arlee, a tribal elder, if he would talk to the children. Johnny came forward and sat on a rock and began:

A long time ago on this river, at the place called Nɫq̓alqʷ (Place of Big, Wide Trees), there lived a young woman. She was a gifted hide-tanner and quillworker—skills that usually only the older women of the Tribe possessed—and she was exceptionally skilled at finding roots and berries when they were ripe and ready for harvest. Even as a young girl she knew, from carefully watching her grandmother, the ways elders would take a little bit of the first foods they gathered after the root feasts and pray, offering a gift for the returning food. The people respected her and said, "She is such a fine young woman. She works hard. She is generous. Everything she does, she does well. And, she is tall and strong, and beautiful. She will make a good wife for one of our young men." They called her Naqey.

Indeed, the young men in the camp liked Naqey very much. They were always offering to carry firewood or water for her, and they often brought her gifts—elk teeth ivories, ermine hides, shells, feathers, and finely decorated hide scrapers. Each young man tried to court her, to win her favor, but Naqey went about her work. She thanked them for their kindness and the gifts, but otherwise she paid little attention to these suitors.

In the middle of the Chokecherry Moon, when all the young women were busy harvesting berries and the men were fishing and preparing for extended hunts, a stranger—a young man named Aay (Bull Trout)—came to visit Naqey. Naqey was picking berries by the creek when she saw Aay. He was different from her people. The way he wore his hair was unfamiliar. She did not recognize his clothing. He wore a smoked buckskin robe painted the color of water with beautiful *yućmn* (red paint) spots with *sčiłt* (white-clay) halos. She admired the uncommon workmanship, which she thought flawless. His earrings, made from iridescent shell, were strange to her too, and very beautiful. He smelled of fresh spring water. "I have come from a lake a great distance to the west of here," he said. She noticed he had great strength and thought him the most handsome man she had ever seen. Immediately she knew she loved this man.

After that, Aay came often to visit Naqey. They spent many hours walking by the river picking berries, talking, and sharing stories of their two peoples. Every morning when Naqey rose, she thought of him, and she would hurry out of camp to the place where they first met to wait for him. When she saw him coming she would say to herself, "*ʔe ni!* How grand he is!" She liked him very much, and their time together was the happiest Naqey had known.

One day she said, "You must stay and show yourself to my parents." But Aay looked away and said, "No, I am too poor. Your people would not like me."

Still, he came every day to visit her, and one day she told her parents about him. But because she had been visiting this man in secret and because he was different, they did not like him and did not want him around their daughter. Her parents went to the leader of the people, and the leader called everyone together. All were in agreement that they disliked Aay. The next time he came, they shunned him. The young men taunted him, and Naqey's parents told him not to visit their daughter anymore. So he left. He was angry at what had happened and at how the people had treated him. Of all the ways the Tribe could show its disapproval, shunning—which meant complete rejection by Naqey's people—was the most serious and insulting. But more difficult than that, Aay's heart was broken with the thought that he might not see Naqey again.

Aay's home was at a place called Nčm̓čmci'netk^w, which means "in dark waters." Today we call this place "Lake Pend Oreille." On the way he spoke with the water in the river: "*K^w ʔiqs nsewłk^wm̓*" ("I'm going to ask of you to follow me"). "*ʔiqs łćim łu sqelix^w tl̓ Nłq'aḷq^w Sewłk^ws*" ("I want to punish the people from the Jocko River").

Water told Aay, "Here is the song for that purpose," and then sang a song.

Later, Aay sang Water's song. As he sang, he could feel its power. Indeed, the song had great power. It made all the water follow him. The Jocko River dried up. The bigger river, too, that the Jocko flowed into, was now nothing but an empty riverbed, a trail of bleached boulders and cobbles. Water's song had dried up all the water—the springs, the creeks, the rivers—all the way to Lake Pend Oreille. Now the young woman's people would have nothing to drink.

The animals, too, became thirsty and left their country. The People could not catch fish or find game. Soon even the food and medicine plants began to dry up. The People's food stores quickly grew low.

The girl told her people, "You mistreated Aay. You were unkind to Aay. That is why he has taken the water with him."

The leader called his advisors together to make a decision about what they should do. They decided the people should make the long walk down the dry riverbed to Lake Pend Oreille to make amends. The journey would take many days.

They gathered what little water they had and packed their dried food into buckskin bags and parfleches and began their journey downstream to where the Jocko joins the Flathead River. They called this place Epł čtet̓ʔú Sčilip, which means "Where the two rivers join and there are wild plums." There, they set up camp, and immediately some of the young men spread out to search for water while others hunted for fresh meat. But they returned with nothing. There was no water, no game. Even the plums had dried hard as rocks.

The second day, they traveled farther down the riverbed and made camp at Čłq̓ʷéẃs, which means, "A small prairie with flat, open land between hills." Here, another big river, the Nmesule, joined the Flathead, but it, too, was dry. The prairie was so parched that clouds of dust rose when the people crossed it. The elders knew they must be brave, and they showed no fear. Again they sent the young men out to hunt for fresh meat and to bring back water. Again the young men returned with nothing.

On the third day they stopped at Nc̓ck̓ʷiʔkʷ (Place of the Elderberries Water), but the elderberries there had dried up. Only a parched wind rattled the dead leaves. The people looked at each other with fear, their throats sore from the dryness.

In the morning they traveled to Sq̓eyɬkʷm (Place of the Sound of Falling Water), but there was no sound of water and no game. The silence there disturbed them greatly, and again the elders encouraged them to remain brave. Together they prayed for water.

On the fifth night they camped at the confluence of the Bull River and Clark Fork, at a place called Nnq̓ʷoƛ̓š (Animals Running through the Woods). This place was still, the trees leafless. Even the bushes along the place where the creek had been were dry.

At Nnenesletkʷ (It Has Two Creeks), where they had camped many times in the past and had always had success hunting elk and picking huckleberries, they found nothing. The place was absent of all living things, and the People felt certain they would soon die of thirst and hunger.

Finally, on the seventh day they reached the place where the river flows into Lake Pend Oreille, a place called Nčm̓m̓cí (Mouth of the River). At first it looked like the lake was dry, but when they looked very hard they could see water far in the distance, and they felt great joy and relief. They thanked the Creator and moved quickly across the dry lakebed to the water's edge, where, for the first time in days, they drank. They went to sleep that night listening to the sounds of the water on the shore.

In the morning they made a canoe from bark and heaped softly tanned buckskins and finely decorated clothing in it. They dressed Naqey in a buckskin dress that the elder women of the camp had made beautiful with quillwork and paint. They placed shell necklaces around her neck and earrings in her ears. They combed and braided her hair and scented her with fragrance. When they had finished, their chief prayed that the gifts might be accepted and that they might now be reconciled with the water, fish, plants, and other animals.

Naqey climbed in the canoe and sat on the buckskin blankets. At once the sky became overcast and the air grew heavy. Rain began to fall, slowly at first, then it poured out of the sky. Springs burst forth and streams started to flow. Lake Pend Oreille began to fill. The People, soaked by rain and full of joy, watched the water in the lake rise and float the canoe. Then they saw Aay in the distance, swimming toward it. When he reached the canoe he climbed in and joined the young woman. The two stood and, smiling, Naqey called to her people: "Ẏetłx̣ʷa, ṁ ʔesya eł x̣stwiĺš. Taqs q̓sip ṁ eł čxʷuymncn" ("Now all is well. I will visit you soon").

Night came, and the people camped at their traditional place on the lakeshore at the edge of the woods, this time with peace and reconciliation in their hearts, knowing they had set things right again. In the morning they left offerings on the lakeshore before beginning their long journey back. All along the way the rivers and streams rushed clear and full. Birds sang and bathed in the water. They saw elk and deer and moose and bear. The plants grew strong. All was well again. All was good.

After a short time Naqey traveled back to the Jocko River and told her people, "I will live at Lake Pend Oreille, in the fish country. The people there are just the same as here, and they live in the same way." This made her people happy.

Later, she returned with her husband, bringing gifts of fish. She told them, "From now on, people here will always be able to catch plenty of fish." She returned a third time to show them her newly born children. After that she went back to Lake Pend Oreille, and her people never saw her again.

That is why every year the bull trout return to the Jocko River to spawn.

When Johnny Arlee had finished, one of the students asked Ms. Howlett if there were any gifts that people could give to the bull trout now, so that the fish could come back to the Jocko River as plentiful as before.

"This Jocko River Restoration Project is a way of giving back," Ms Howlett said. "It is our gift to the bull trout and to the plants and animals that live on the Jocko; it is our way of giving back for all that they have given us. Maybe Mr. Barfoot can tell us about some of the things the Tribes are doing to restore the river."

"One of the things we are doing," Mr. Barfoot said, "is that in some places, where the river needs help, we are reconnecting the river channel to the floodplain so each spring the river can replenish the groundwater that flows beneath the floodplain. Then, in the summer when the weather is hot and dry and the river is low, that same groundwater can flow back into the river. Because the groundwater is cold it will help keep the river cold."

"We are replanting native trees and shrubs on the floodplain that shade the river, which also helps keep it cold. To clean the water we are stabilizing and replanting unstable stream banks and fixing forest roads that have been eroding and adding sediment to the river.

"We are also managing cattle in a way that reduces the impact they have on the stream: carefully planning when and for how long they can graze along the river, developing springs away from the river where they can drink, and fencing sensitive riparian areas. We are working with ranchers and farmers to minimize the amount of irrigation water they take from the river.

"In places where the river has been severely damaged, we are rebuilding the river channel and floodplain to make more habitats; in other words, we are making the river more complex. We do this by adding river meanders, side-channels, and large logs and rocks to the stream to provide places for fish to rest and hide. Our tree and shrub planting is helping to make the riparian area more complex.

"We are removing barriers—like culverts and irrigation diversions—to connect habitat so that native fish can repopulate areas where they once lived. At the same time, we are taking steps to control non-native species. And we are reconnecting the river to the floodplain by removing levees and dikes."

Johnny Arlee rose again to speak.

"The most important thing we can all do," he said, "is be careful in how we treat the river, making sure that whatever we do, we do nothing to harm it.

"It is our tradition to give thanks for the things the river gives us and to return something in exchange. As the elders tell us, a long time ago the spiritual leaders would send the young men into the mountains where the streams began. The young men gave blessings upon each stream for the abundance of clean water for people, for plants, and for animals that depend upon water for their livelihood.

"So the most important gift we can give the river and bull trout is to take care of them and protect them. This is your responsibility for the future."

A Note to Parents and Teachers

by Germaine White

"It is there in the water—that is where there were many animals, fish, and other things. By that, we were wealthy from the water." Mitch Smallsalmon's words, like those of all of our elders, are at the center of our understanding of the natural world and our understanding of the consequences of change. Our work on this education project is based first and foremost on what the elders have told us about the Jocko River and the community of life it supports, and how that community and the river itself have been altered over the last one hundred years. They know what we have lost because they have witnessed the changes.

As a child I learned Mitch's lesson from my dad. I followed him up and down the creek above Hammer's Dam as he fished. He fished every chance he had: after work, on weekends, during holidays. The creek was quiet and shaded by cedars and was a cool sanctuary from hot summer days. It was also a cool sanctuary from the hectic life of school, chores, and other responsibilities. It was a place where time stood still, and I felt happy. By taking me fishing, my father taught me that the natural world can set your life right again. Now, when the force of responsibilities from daily life presses on me, I return to the comfort of a long walk beside a cool, quiet creek. Those experiences have led me to want what the elders have taught from time immemorial: we want to protect and enhance natural places for ourselves and so we can pass their gifts on to our children and grandchildren.

The landscape we inherited is in large part the product of tribal values—of countless generations of our ancestors protecting and caring for the land, the water, and its fish and wildlife. Agnes Vanderburg, Joe Eneas, Clarence Woodcock, and Louise McDonald were some of our elders who maintained this vision. It is ultimately a vision of hope for our children. They knew the importance of clean water and healthy streams. They knew native fish were worth saving—not just for them but for future generations.

Our elders taught us these lessons, and now it is our turn. It is our turn to conserve and care for water and bull trout. It is our turn—indeed it is our responsibility—to pass on to our children what the elders taught us: that the land has been good to us and we must in turn be good to the land. When you take from it, you should never take more than you need, and you should always leave something of equal or greater value in return.

It is our hope this book and the accompanying educational materials will help do this, specifically that they will help young people understand the importance of mending a river that has undergone one hundred years of unnatural change, a river with warming temperatures and a declining bull trout population. It is our hope they will help young people want to protect and care for the river in the future and, perhaps most important, that they will encourage an understanding and adoption of the basic principle of reciprocity, a principle that for millennia governed our ancestors' relations with the river.

That is our hope, but we do not expect that these (or any) educational materials can accomplish this by themselves. Parents and teachers play a much more important role. Taking a child on a fishing or camping trip or a hike or simply spending quiet time exploring a natural setting, can imprint a love of the natural world that lasts a lifetime. We believe these experiences have the greatest impact on the way our children think about and care for the land, now and in the future. Teachers, by providing opportunities for experiential learning and meditation in outdoor settings, can also have an enormous effect. Experiences in nature are among the most precious gifts we have to offer our children.

The theme of this book is reciprocity, that is, when we take from nature we are obligated to give something of equal or greater value in return. As the students in the story learn, a wonderful example of this principle is the Tribes' Jocko River Restoration Project. The scope of the project is unparalleled. It seeks to restore, to varying degrees, the river's own natural processes, its native floodplain vegetation, its hydrology, and its corridors for the movement of animals. In short, to reestablish, as much as we can, the natural processes and conditions that existed before the river was disturbed.

Restoring the Jocko is an attempt by our generation to give something back to a river that has given so much to us and our ancestors. In doing so we hope to renew and sustain our relationship with the river and its native species, especially bull trout. In the process we are restoring to our children part of their cultural and natural resource inheritance. In a very real sense we are giving them hope for the future.

We have great challenges ahead of us, but we have been given an extraordinary gift—Bull Trout's Gift—and now it is our turn to give something in return.

The Artist

Sashay Camel creates her artwork on the Flathead Indian Reservation in western Montana. A member of the Confederated Salish and Kootenai Tribes, she has painted for a number of years. Her work includes illustrations for the American Indian College Fund. She works seasonally at the National Bison Range in Moiese, Montana, and lives with her husband and two children in St. Ignatius. This is her first book.

The Storyteller

Johnny Arlee was raised by his grandparents with Salish as his first language. He has worked tirelessly throughout his life to pass on the traditional culture and way of life of the Salish and Pend d'Oreille people. In the 1970s and 1980s Johnny played a key role in developing the Salish Pend d'Oreille Culture Committee into a nationally respected tribal cultural institution. Johnny is the author of four books: Coyote Stories of the Montana Salish Indians; Mali Nqnaqs: The Story of a Mean Little Old Lady; Over a Century of Moving to the Drum: The Salish Powwow Tradition on the Flathead Indian Reservation; and Beaver Steals Fire: A Salish Coyote Story. He has served as technical advisor, actor, and scripting consultant on several feature-length motion pictures, including the classic Jeremiah Johnson. Johnny served as cultural advisor for the Salish and Kootenai Tribal Health Department, and presently serves as Salish language translator and transcriber for the Kalispel Tribe of Indians at Usk, Washington. He lives in Arlee, Montana.

The Bull Trout Education Project

This book is one part of a larger bull trout restoration and protection project. The project includes an integrated set of educational materials that focus not only on the Tribes' restoration and management efforts but also on bull trout, their habitat needs, and their historic relationship to the Salish, Kootenai, and Pend d'Oreille people. The materials also discuss key hydrological and ecological concepts that are fundamental to restoration; the changes that have occurred in aquatic and riparian habitats as a result of one hundred years of agriculture, irrigation, and grazing practices; and how and why restoration is occurring in the Jocko watershed. Materials produced include:

- A storybook for students, combining key hydrological and ecological concepts that are fundamental to bull trout restoration and protection and a Salish story told by Johnny Arlee;

- An interactive DVD designed primarily for middle and high school students;

- A web site targeting the general public for anyone seeking information about the Tribes' restoration activities on the Jocko River and the Bull Trout Education Project;

- A field journal for students; and

- A curriculum guide for educators.

Pronunciation Guide for Salish and Pend d'Oreille Dialects as Written in the International Phonetic Alphabet

January 2010
Salish–Pend d'Oreille Culture Committee

Salish–Pend d'Oreille Alphabet

Aa Áá Cc Ċċ Čč Č̓č̓ Ee Éé Hh Ii Íí Kk K̓k̓ Kʷkʷ K̓ʷk̓ʷ Ll Łł Ĺl̓ Ḻḻ X̌ƛ̓
Mm M̓m̓ Ṃṃ Nn N̓n̓ Ṇṇ Oo Óó Pp Ṗṗ Qq Q̓q̓ Qʷqʷ Q̓ʷq̓ʷ Ss Šš Tt T̓t̓ Uu Úú
Ww W̓w̓ X̣x̣ Xx X̱x̱ Xʷxʷ X̱ʷx̱ʷ Yy Y̓y̓ ʔ

The Vowels

a the vowel sound in the English words far, car, and are.

e the vowel sound in the English words end, yes, and wed. If there is an e at the end of a word, it must be pronounced. In Salish every letter is pronounced; there are no silent e's in any words.

i the vowel sound in the English words see and week.

o the sound between the vowel sounds in the English words road and bought.

u the vowel sound in the English words cool, moo, and boo.

55

The Stops

c a sound similar to the English ts sound at the end of the words cats and rats.

č the soft ch sound in the English word church.

k the k sound in the English word key.

k^w the k sound pronounced with the mouth rounded. It is similar to the start of the English word quick but is made slightly further forward in the mouth.

p a sound like the English p in the words paper and people.

q a sound similar to the k sound but pronounced farther back in the mouth or throat.

q^w the q sound pronounced with the mouth rounded. It is similar to the start of the English word queen but is made slightly farther back in the mouth or throat.

t the t sound in the English words to, hot, and at.

The Glottalized Stops

ċ the c (ts) sound pronounced with glottalization (harder).

č̓ the č (ch) sound pronounced with glottalization.

k̓^{w} the k^w sound pronounced with glottalization.

ƛ̓ a clicking type of sound that combines the ŧ and the l sounds. This is called a lambda.

ṗ the p sound pronounced with glottalization, producing a slight pop.

q̓ the q sound pronounced with glottalization.

q̓^{w} the q̓ sound pronounced with the mouth rounded.

ṫ the t sound pronounced with glottalization, producing a slight pop.

The Fricatives

s the s sound in the English words say and yes.

š the sh sound in the English words shut, push, and wish.

h the h sound in the English word hot.

ł a sound made by pushing air along the sides of the mouth with the tongue behind the teeth. It is called a barred L or an unvoiced L.

x̣ a friction-like sound produced in the same area of the mouth as the q. (To learn this sound, begin by producing a sound much like softly clearing the throat.)

x̣ʷ the x̣ sound made with the mouth rounded.

xʷ the wh sound in the English word whoosh, made with the mouth rounded.

The Resonants

l a sound similar to the English l.

m a sound like the English m.

n a sound like the English n.

w a sound like the English w.

y a sound like the English y in the words yes, pay, and yarn.

The Glottalized Resonants

l̓ the l sound pronounced with glottalization.

m̓ the m sound pronounced with glottalization.

n̓ the n sound pronounced with glottalization.

w̓ the w sound pronounced with glottalization.

y̓ the y sound pronounced with glottalization.

The Glottal Stop

? a sound made by simply closing and opening the vocal chords. It abruptly cuts off or starts a sound, and is used before or after a vowel in some words. It is similar to the break in the middle of the English expression uh-huh, indicating no.

Long Vowels and Long Consonants

In words with double consonants, each consonant is pronounced separately.

In words with double vowels, each vowel is pronounced separately. This pronunciation makes the vowel sound longer.